THINGS I'D DO

(but just for you)

JACK SJOGREN

CHRONICLE BOOKS
SAN FRANCISCO

for Hal

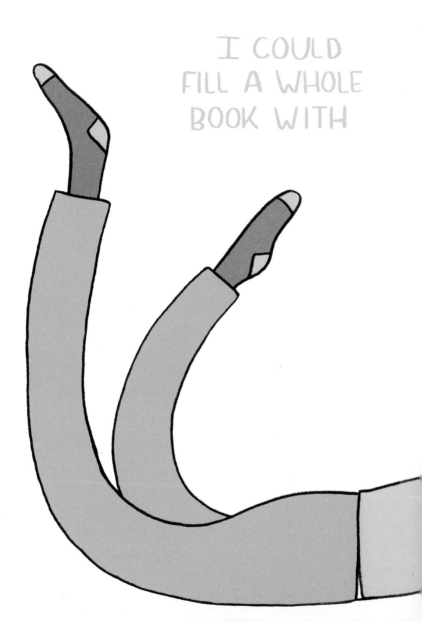

I COULD
FILL A WHOLE
BOOK WITH

I'D CALL
YOU UP

just
hear

I'D CLEAR OUT
MY ENTIRE
SCHEDULE FOR YOU

I'D GIVE YOU
a reasonable
AMOUNT OF TIME
TO GET READY

I'D COOK
YOU DINNER

and I'd
understand
if you weren't
quite hungry

I'D CRACK
YOUR BACK

whenever we say
hello or
goodbye

I'D GROW
A BEARD

to keep
you warm

I'D WEAR
ALL YOUR CLOTHES

so you
have options
when we go out

I WOULD DRIVE
THROUGH DOWNTOWN

at 5 p.m. for you

I'D SHIELD
YOUR EYES
FROM THE
SCARY PARTS

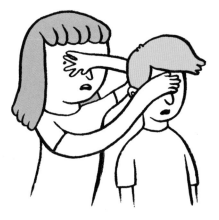

and bravely
describe them
as they occur

I'D SIT THROUGH THE

The

Even though I know

CREDITS WITH YOU

End

there won't be any bloopers

I'D WRITE YOU TOASTS FOR ANY WEDDINGS YOU ATTEND

"TO THE HAPPY COUPLE, who let us swim in their pool"

I'D TELL YOUR WEIRD UNCLE

to buzz off

I WOULD

KILL

FOR YOU

on the
dance floor

I'D BAKE YOU
A CAKE

YOU

EXIST

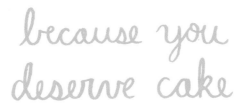

because you deserve cake

I'D DO
THE DISHES
FOR YOU

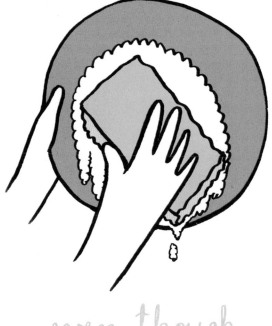

even though
its your turn,
but whatever

I'D SET ASIDE
THE CROSSWORDS
FOR YOU

FOR YOU,
I'D FIND A

wretched
monster...

... AND
MAKE
IT
OUR
FRIEND

I'D MAKE YOU
COUPONS

ONE COUPON
GOOD FOR
ENDLESS
COUPONS

so you'll
always have
a good deal
on my services

I'D LEARN
TO CLIMB
FOR YOU

because calling
the fire department
can be embarrassing

I WOULD WRITE A 50-PAGE
ESSAY FOR YOU

on an unfamiliar
word processor

I WOULD PRETEND TO BE YOU

I would
write you
doctor's notes

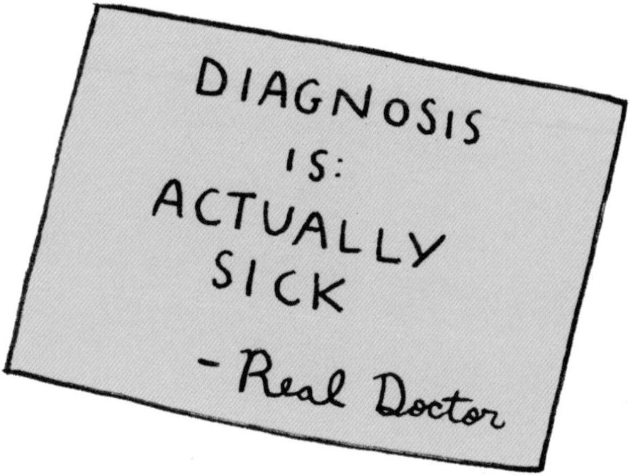
DIAGNOSIS IS: ACTUALLY SICK
-Real Doctor

I'D REMIND YOU

that you're lucky
to have a job

but also that

YOU ARE NOT
YOUR JOB

I'D
TEACH
YOU
HOW
TO
DANCE...

"THE PICKLE JAR STRUGGLE"

I'D REORGANIZE YOUR BOOKS

BOOK OF TINY HATS

HOW TO FALL OUT OF LOVE w/ YOUR BARISTA

SPORTS, AND WHY

GETTING THE POINT: A GUIDE TO KNIVES

ONE PICTURE OF A HORSE

DON'T SWEAT ANY STUFF

How To Be Goth

however you'd like

I WOULD ASSEMBLE YOUR NEW FURNITURE

my way

I'D MAKE YOU
A TINY HAT

in case
your hat
gets cold

I WOULD CUT OFF THE CRUST FOR YOU

(I secretly love the crust)

I'D FINISH OFF
YOUR PLATE

it's all good
to me

I'D WAKE YOU UP

with donuts

I'D FIND YOUR
FOURTH GRADE
TEACHER
and tell them

just to quit
for you

I'D START POSITIVE RUMORS ABOUT YOU

I WOULD
COMPLETELY RUIN
A BATCH OF
COOKIES FOR YOU

'cause I know
you like 'em burnt

I'D BE
THE LEGS
IN OUR
TAG-TEAM
COSTUME

"giant detective"

I'D CREATE NEW

curse words

FOR YOU

SO YOU'LL ALWAYS
BE ON THE
CUTTING EDGE
OF VULGARITY

I'D BINGE-WATCH
YOUR FAVORITE SHOW

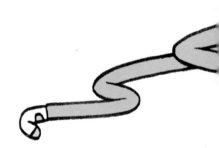

to catch up
for the
season premiere

I'D PRETEND
TO BE
A PUPPY

in case you need
to cry it out

WHENEVER YOU ASKED

I'D SHAKE THE
SAND OFF
YOUR TOWEL

what's a
little sand
in my eyes?

I'D PUT SUNSCREEN
ON YOUR
HARD-TO-REACH
ZONE

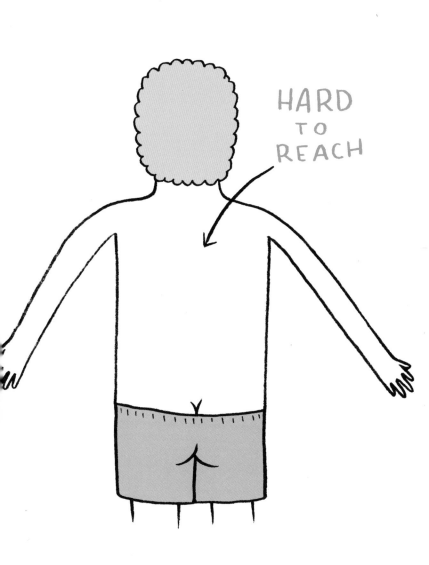

I'd clean your
WINDOWS

I'D MAKE IT SEEM
LIKE YOU'RE HOME

when you go
out of town

I'D CURATE
THE BEST VIEWS
OF THE CITY...

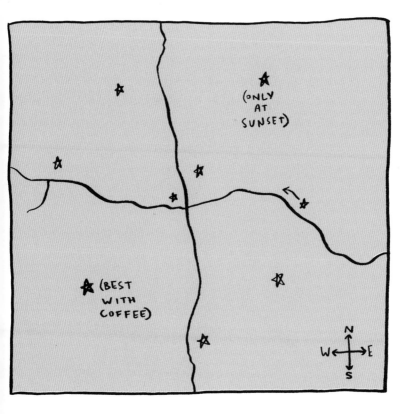

a guided tour

I'D REMIND YOU TO

WITH

ALL

THESE

THINGS,

I
MEAN
TO
SAY
THAT...

I'D DO
anything

FOR YOU

(but just

for you)

Endless thanks to my family.
I couldn't be me without you.

Special thanks to Hallie Bateman,
Michael Cochran and family,
Caleb Groh and family,
Emily Henry and family, Joey Cook,
Nigel Reyes, Jeff Pianki,
Caroline Tompkins, Tuesday Bassen,
Chris Rogness, Michael Seymour Blake,
Adam Carpenter, Phil McAndrew,
Jesse Moynihan, everyone else I love,
and Olive the dog.

Jack Sjorgen is a cartoonist
in Los Angeles, where he can often
be found drawing, giggling, and
drinking too much coffee.

For more info, visit jacksjorgen.com or
follow him on social media at
@sjorgenjack

Library of Congress Cataloging-in-Publication Data available.

ISBN 978-1-4521-5638-5

Manufactured in China.

Chronicle Books LLC
680 Second Street
San Francisco, CA 94107
www.chroniclebooks.com

10 9 8 7 6 5 4 3 2 1